Water

Use less – save more

100 WATER-SAVING
TIPS FOR THE HOME

JON CLIFT & AMANDA CUTHBERT

Chelsea Green Publishing Company
White River Junction, Vermont

First published in 2006 by Green Books
Foxhole, Dartington
Totnes, Devon, TQ9 6EB, UK

First Chelsea Green printing July, 2007

Text design concept by Julie Martin, jmartin1@btinternet.com

Printed on 100-percent postconsumer-waste recycled paper

Printed in Canada

10 9 8 7 6 5 4 3 2 1   07 08 09 10

Library of Congress Cataloging-in-Publication Data
Clift, Jon.
  Water, use less—save more : 100 energy-saving tips for the
home / Jon Clift & Amanda Cuthbert.
     p. cm.
  Includes bibliographical references.
  ISBN 978-1-933392-73-8
  1. Water conservation. 2. Dwellings. I. Cuthbert, Amanda.
II. Title. III. Title: 100 water-saving tips for the home.

  TD388.C58 2007
  644'.6—dc22

                          2007021273

Chelsea Green Publishing Company
P.O. Box 428
White River Junction, VT 05001
(802) 295-6300
www.chelseagreen.com

Contents

Introduction

Introduction

Water. We all need it, we can't live without it, and we are using more and more of it.

Although we appear to have plenty of rain in the United States, our water resources are under pressure. We use 127% more water today than we did in 1950.

● Our population is growing
● Our climate is changing
● Our lifestyle demands more and more water

Quite simply, we are consuming too much. Our demand for water increases yearly, to the extent that no matter what the water companies do, eventually they will not be able to keep up. Water also requires huge amounts of energy, both to treat it and pump it to our houses, so our thirst for water is damaging our planet in more ways than one.

The good news is that there are many simple things we can do at home and at work to reduce our consumption of water. As well as helping to secure our water supply both for ourselves and for future generations, by doing these things we also benefit in many other ways.

By cutting down our water use, we can:

- Save money, especially if on a water meter
- Reduce the possibility of water shortages and summer water rationing
- Reduce emissions of greenhouse gases responsible for climate change
- Reduce the amount of energy and chemicals used in the treatment and pumping of water
- Reduce damage to wildlife habitats in wetlands and rivers
- Reduce the fall in groundwater levels, thereby reducing stress on woodlands

Here are 100 water-saving tips for the home and garden – if each one of us does just one of them, we can help reduce water shortages, water rationing, and our impact on the environment.

We use 127% more water than we did in 1950.

How much water do you use?

How much water do you use?

Are you letting money flow down the drain? Find out how much water you use: how much is it costing you?

Bath	40 gallons
5-minute shower	10 gallons
5-minute power shower	20 gallons
Brushing teeth with tap running	2 gallons/min
Brushing teeth with tap off	.25 gallon
One toilet flush	3 gallons
Other water use (drinking, cooking, etc.)	7 gallons
Washing machine	40 gallons
Dishwasher	10 gallons
Washing car with bucket	3 gallons
Hose/sprinkler	140 gallons/hour

The kitchen

The kitchen

About 95% of the water that gets delivered to our houses goes down the drain.

1 Never leave a tap running.

2 Use a bowl to wash vegetables or to wash and rinse plates.

3 Use the leftover water to water your garden or house plants, provided it is not too soapy (see also *The garden*, page 41).

Overall, only 3% of the water entering the average home is actually used as 'drinking' water.

4 Store drinking water in a jug in the refrigerator, rather than waiting for the tap to run cold.

5 Fix that leaky tap.

> Leaky faucets that drip at the rate of one drop per second can waste up to 2,700 gallons of water each year.

6 If you are making a hot drink, fill the kettle with only as much water as you need. You will save energy as well as water.

> Most of us couldn't survive for a week without water. Health experts figure that we need at least 6–8 glasses of water every day to keep us fit and healthy and aid our concentration.

7 Tap water is around 500 times cheaper than bottled water—chill it in the fridge and see if you can taste the difference!

> A gallon of bottled drinking water
> can be more expensive than a
> gallon of gas.

Dishwashing

8   Only use a dishwasher if you have a full load. If you just
   have a few things to wash, use a bowl.

9   While waiting for your water to run hot, collect the cold
   water and use it on your plants.

10 If you have to replace your dishwasher with a new one,
   choose a water-efficient model.

> A water-efficient dishwasher will
> use as little as 4 gallons per wash
> cycle, whereas some older models
> use up to 13 gallons per cycle.

Waste

11 Garbage disposals use a considerable amount of water.
   Start composting – put the vegetable peelings in your
   compost bin.

12 Avoid pouring used grease, fat, or cooking oil down your kitchen sink or drain, as these quickly cool and solidify and the fatty deposits build up and cause blockages. This is generally noticed only during periods of heavy rain, when blocked sewers can overflow onto gardens and into properties. Put all your used fat and grease to good use—mix it up into a 'bird cake' with some nuts, seeds, and raisins and hang it out for the garden birds to feed on. **www.rspb.org.uk/feedthebirds**

Laundry

13 Hand-wash small amounts of clothes in a bowl.

14 Only use your washing machine with a full load; half-load programs are generally neither water- nor energy-efficient.

> **Older washing machines can use up to 40 gallons per cycle, whereas new ones use about 27 gallons.**

15 When you next replace your washing machine, check out the amount of water it uses and buy a more efficient one. Look for appliances labeled with the Energy Star® label, which indicates that the product has met strict energy efficiency guidelines.

The bathroom

The bathroom

16 Check all the taps on sinks, baths, and toilets for leaks or drips.

17 Don't keep the tap running while cleaning your teeth; use a mug of water.

> **A running tap can use as much as 4 gallons of water in the time it takes to clean your teeth.**

18 Have a shower instead of a bath. But if you use a power shower, beware: they can use as much water as a bath if you shower for more than five minutes.

19 Put the plug in the drain and only run as much water as you need when washing.

20 Attach a flow regulator to your shower.

21 Attach a water-saving tap.

22 Bathe with a friend.

The toilet

The toilet

Over a quarter of all the clean, drinkable water you use in your home is used to flush the toilets.

23 Remember the rhyme: "If it's yellow let it mellow, if it's brown flush it down." You will save a lot of water!

24 If you have an old toilet, you can reduce the amount of water it uses by putting a "displacement device" in the tank. Use small plastic bottles filled with water or a displacement bag designed for toilet tanks. Displacement bags may be available free from your local water department or can be purchased from a hardware store.

Older toilets can use 3 gallons of clean water with every flush, while new toilets use as little as 1 gallon.

25 Avoid flushing anything down the toilet that has not previously passed though your digestive system, apart from toilet paper – it's a waste of water and might block the sewer. Bag it and bin it.

26 When you are buying a new toilet, look for a dual-flush toilet, or a low-flush toilet, which uses only 1.6 gallons per flush.

> **Many people in the world exist on 3 gallons of water day or less. We can use that amount in one flush of the toilet.**

27 Choose a slimline toilet rather than a full-size toilet; they use a lot less water per flush.

28 Why not pee into a container and use this nitrogen-rich liquid to speed up the decomposition of the contents of your compost bin? Just pour it on.

29 If you have enough space, or are building a new house, how about making a composting toilet?
www.compostingtoilet.org

The garden

The garden

Watering

> The average roof collects about 22,500 gallons of rain a year – enough to fill 450 50-gallon rain barrels with free water.

30 Use a rain barrel to collect the rainwater from your roof, rather than wasting treated drinking water on your garden. Some water companies either provide them free or at a reduced price. You can also build your own.

31 Use two rain barrels or more and link them so that when one is full the surplus water is diverted into the others.

32 Keep your rain barrels covered to avoid evaporation.

33 Put a gutter and rain barrel on your greenhouse or garden shed.

The oceans and seas of the world contain 97% of all our water, but it's salty. With the polar ice caps containing another 2%, there is very little fresh water left for us to use.

34 Keep your gutters clear so you don't waste all the water that falls on your roof. Collect it all in your rain barrel(s).

35 Use a watering can to water your garden; hoses and sprinklers waste a tremendous amount of water, and their use may be limited during a water shortage (check with your water company).

36 If you do use a hose, fit a trigger nozzle at the end so you can turn the water on and off easily – don't leave it running unnecessarily.

37 Avoid using sprinklers. Trickle-irrigation and drip-irrigation systems help reduce water use and supply adequate water to plants.

A garden hose or sprinkler can use almost as much water in an hour as an average family of four uses in one day.

38 Check the weather forecast before you start watering – it may be going to rain soon.

39 Water your plants early in the morning or during the evening when it is cool, so that less water is lost through evaporation.

40 Avoid watering when it is windy, as this increases the evaporation rate.

41 Make your plants more drought-resistant by watering them occasionally but thoroughly – rather than little and often, which encourages shallow rooting.

> **Our wetlands are drying out. A recent survey found that over 70% were in an unfavorable condition.**

42 Direct the water to the base of the plants and give the roots a good soak. A couple of times a week should be sufficient, even when the weather is hot.

43 Make it easy to water near the base of the plant by cutting the bottom off a plastic bottle and burying the neck in the ground near the roots.

44 Create a natural, untended garden for wildflowers and wildlife. It won't need watering.

The garden ● 41

Gray water

45 Use 'gray water' (waste water from baths, sinks, etc.) to water your garden flowers, but don't water salad crops or other vegetables with it – 'gray water' can contain fecal coliforms, which might cause illness if ingested.

46 Avoid using 'gray water' that has a lot of strong detergents in it, as this might damage your plants.

47 'Gray water' is best used soon after collection; don't store it for much longer than 24 hours, as it might get smelly.

48 Don't use 'gray water' on pot plants, as they will start to smell unpleasant, and detergent levels can build up in the pot.

49 If your bath is on a higher level than the garden, you could siphon the bath water directly onto the garden or into a rain barrel.

50 You can use the water from your washing machine by attaching a hose to the washing machine outlet pipe. Collect the used water when the machine is discharging and use it to water the garden.

Plants

By using less water we can help to reduce the fall in groundwater levels, thereby reducing stress on woodlands.

51 Choose drought-resistant bedding plants – try African or French marigolds, petunias, geraniums, and alyssum.

52 Choose perennial plants that need little watering, such as campanula, heuchera (coral flower), and aquilegia.

53 Choose flowers and shrubs that positively enjoy dry, hot conditions, such as evening primrose, buddleia, rock rose, thyme, and lavender.

54 Create shade with ground-cover plants, trellises, or hedges to help prevent evaporation of moisture from the soil.

55 Move your potted plants to a shaded part of the garden during hot, dry periods.

Trees are about 75% water.

Vegetables

56 Group your vegetables together according to their water needs when you plan your vegetable garden.

57 Crops with plenty of leaves – such as lettuce, peas, runner beans, tomatoes, potatoes, salad onions, cauliflower, and broccoli – require the most water.

58 Squash, zucchini, and cucumbers need regular watering once their fruit begins to swell.

59 Vegetables such as corn, broad beans, and French beans will survive with less watering, although their yields will be lower.

60 Root crops such as beets, turnips, and carrots, together with asparagus, are the most drought-resistant. However, root crops will become hard and woody if they get too dry.

Check your soil by digging a spadeful of earth near the plant – only water if the earth is dry at the bottom of the hole.

Compost

61 Get composting: Instead of throwing away all your garden waste, vegetable peelings, paper, and cardboard, compost them.

62 Build up the organic content of your soil by using plenty of manure and compost. This will increase its ability to retain moisture.

63 Plant vegetables close together. This will shade the soil and reduce moisture loss.

Some experts estimate that more than 50 percent of landscape water use goes to waste due to evaporation or runoff caused by overwatering.

Mulch

64 Help to reduce moisture loss and keep the soil cool by using your compost to form a layer of mulch on top of the soil. A mulch also suppresses weeds and feeds your plants.

65 You can also make a mulch using other organic materials such as manure, hay or straw, a thin layer of grass cuttings, or locally produced bark or wood chippings.

66 Mulching with your compost will also build up the organic content of the soil, increasing its ability to hold moisture.

67 Keep the spaces between crops well-mulched, using compost, grass cuttings, straw, or hay.

> **By using less water we can help reduce emissions of greenhouse gases which are responsible for climate change.**

68 Place organic mulch into the planting holes of thirsty plants, such as sweet peas, peas, beans, squash, and melons, before planting out. This will improve the ability of the soil to hold moisture around the roots.

69 Control weeds during hot weather by mulching rather than hoeing. Don't disturb the soil.

70 Plant vegetables such as potatoes under a mulch, rather than ridging them.

71 Don't bring moist soil to the surface by hoeing or digging – mulch instead.

72 Use old tea leaves or tea bags as a mulch – particularly for roses, which love cold tea.

73 Use old blankets, carpets, or weighted-down layers of cardboard or newspaper on top of the soil to conserve moisture and reduce the amount of watering you need to do in the hot dry summer months.

74 If you have a heavy clay soil, work in some sharp sand or grit in addition to some organic matter to improve water retention. This will reduce the possibility of the soil cracking in dry weather.

By using less water we can help reduce damage to wildlife habitats in wetlands and rivers.

Lawns

75 Let the grass grow longer on your lawns. Cutting it short encourages growth, which needs lots of water.

76 Adjust your lawnmower before you use it so that it cuts higher. Longer lawns last longer!

77 Aerate and spike lawns early in the season to promote deep roots.

78 Don't overfeed your lawn; this encourages excessive growth and requires lots of water.

79 When you cut your lawn, leave the cuttings on it. This will reduce moisture loss and return nutrients to the soil. (If your lawn is really overgrown, compost the first cut.)

Ponds

80 Plant a tree or a large shrub beside your pond to give shade and reduce evaporation.

Garden ponds can lose a lot of water through evaporation on hot days.

81 Floating plants such as water lilies also help reduce evaporation and provide shade for fish and other pond life. Cover at least half the pond with these floating plants to provide a large shaded area.

82 If you are filling a new pond, your plants and fish will be much happier if you use rainwater instead of tap water.

Pipes, taps and tanks

> **Just one dripping overflow can waste over 20 gallons a day – a whole bathful of water.**

83 Insulate all outside taps and pipes to prevent the water from freezing inside them when it is cold and causing burst or leaking pipes.

84 If outside taps are not being used during the winter months, isolate them completely if you can by turning them off at the valve and draining off any water left in them.

85 Check the overflow pipes from your toilet tanks and water storage tanks on your roof to see if any are dripping.

86 Insulate your water pipes and tanks in the attic. Pipes are best insulated by placing them underneath the attic insulation, which allows some heat from the house to reach them and protects them from frost.

Swimming Pools

87 Place an insulated cover over your pool when it is not being used to help prevent water loss through evaporation.

88 Check swimming pools frequently for leaks.

The car

The car

> It takes about 70 gallons of water
> to produce I gallon of gas.

89 Wash your car at home rather than at a car wash.

> It takes about 120,000 gallons of
> water to produce a small car.

90 Wash your car using a sponge and a bucket and some
soap. It works just as well and uses much less water than
a hose or a pressure washer.

> It takes about 35 gallons of water
> to produce a bicycle.

91 Wash your car less often.

And more ...

And more ...

92 If you have a water meter, check for leaks. Make sure no water is being used in your house and garden, then see if the meter is going round; if it is, you have a leak.

93 Have a water meter installed – you will certainly use less water, and installation is free.

> **The average household uses about 15% less water when a water meter is installed.**

94 Make sure everybody in your home knows where your main water valve is and how to work it. Use it to turn the water off if you have a leak.

95 Check the main water valve occasionally to make sure it works – turn the water supply off, try a tap in the house; no water should come out. If there is a problem with your valve, contact your water company.

96 Keep the telephone number of a plumber handy for emergencies.

97 Think before you buy. Most products have to be
manufactured, which consumes huge amounts of water.

> **Far more water is used in
> manufacturing than in our homes.**

98 If you see a water leak or a burst pipe when you are out
and about, tell the water company.

99 Install a rainwater-harvesting system.
http://rainwaterharvesting.tamu.edu

> **Simply installing dual-flush toilets,
> buying water-efficient appliances,
> and using low-flow taps and
> showers can reduce your water
> consumption by about 25%.**

100 Spread the word!

How does your water get to your home?

Collection

All the water you get from your taps starts off by falling from the sky as rain, hail or snow. It is then collected, stored, cleaned, and made safe to drink before being pumped to your house.

Water is taken from rivers, streams, reservoirs, and from deep wells (boreholes) that collect water that has soaked deep into the ground.

Cleaning

This water is then cleaned and treated. First the water is passed through a huge sieve that catches and removes large bits of debris. Then combinations of chemical and physical processes are used to remove the remaining impurities.

To make this water safe to drink, it must be cleansed of any remaining harmful germs or bacteria. This is done by either disinfecting the water with chlorine or ozone, or by treating the water with ultraviolet light.

Storage and delivery

Clean drinking water is now pumped from the water-treatment works and put in covered storage tanks. These are higher than the area they serve, so that the water flows with enough pressure through the pipes to your taps.

The water mains carry the water to just outside your house. From here a service pipe connects the water mains to your house, usually with a valve. This valve is generally found underneath a cover in the pavement and allows you, or your water company, to turn off the water for repairs or maintenance.

You may also have another valve inside your house, probably underneath the kitchen sink, which you can use if you need to repair your household plumbing.

Water –
a global view

Water – a global view

Much of the world already faces acute water shortages – from the poor areas of Central Asia, where rivers and lakes have shrunk or dried up, to the wealthy southwestern states of the United States, where the once mighty Colorado River now no longer even reaches the sea.

China is just one example: due to a rapidly expanding population and economy, currently over 200 cities, including the capital, Beijing, face crucial water shortages. Here the groundwater level has been dropping by about 6 feet every year, and now over a third of the city's wells have dried up.

An estimated 25 million refugees are displaced annually by contamination of rivers and river basins, more than are forced to flee from war zones. By 2025 there will be another 2 billion more people requiring food and water.

We are very lucky in the United States. Currently we have enough water for everybody, provided we look after this precious resource – although a growing population and climate change will undoubtedly place an increasing strain on our water supplies. Just a few of the measures suggested in this book can make a lot of difference, and also save you money.

Conserve water – it's all we have.

Resources

Resources

Action Water

Action Water is a small charity in the UK helping people in developing countries to gain access to safe drinking water and regain a degree of independence.

Phone: +44 (0)1209 210567
Website: **www.actionwater.org.uk**

The American Water Works Association (AWWA)

The AWWA is an international, nonprofit, scientific, and educational society dedicated to the improvement of water quality and supply.

AWWA, 6666 W. Quincy Ave., Denver, CO 80235
Phone: (800) 926-7337
Website: **www.awwa.org**

Environmental Protection Agency (EPA) Office of Water

The EPA enforces federal clean water and safe drinking water laws, provides support for municipal wastewater treatment plants, and takes part in pollution prevention efforts aimed at protecting watersheds and sources of drinking water.

1200 Pennsylvania Avenue, N.W.,
Washington, D.C. 20460
Website: **www.epa.gov/water**

Energy Star®

ENERGY STAR® is a joint program of the U.S. Environmental Protection Agency and the U.S. Department of Energy and provides ratings and advice for energy efficiency. See the section on products for specific information on dishwashers and clothes washers.

1200 Pennsylvania Avenue, N.W.,
Washington, D.C. 20460 Phone: (888) 782-7937
Website: **www.energystar.gov**

The National Association of Regulatory Utility Commissioners (NARUC)

Through its Water Committee, NARUC works to protect public health by ensuring safe drinking water and protecting ground water.

1101 Vermont Avenue, N.W., Washington, DC 20005
Phone: (202) 898-2200
Website: **www.naruc.org**

Royal Society for the Protection of Birds (RSPB)

For further information on using cooking fats and greases to feed garden birds, visit the RSBP Website.

The Lodge, Sandy, Bedfordshire, SG19 2DL, UK
Phone: +44 (0)1767 680551
Website: **www.rspb.org.uk/feedthebirds**

WaterAid America

WaterAid is an international non-governmental organization dedicated exclusively to the provision of safe domestic water, sanitation and hygiene education to the world's poorest people.

232 Madison Avenue, Suite 1202, New York, NY 10016
Phone: (212) 683-0430
Website: **www.wateraid.org**

United States Geological Survey (USGS)

The mission of the USGS Water Resource Discipline is to provide reliable, impartial, timely information that is needed to understand the nation's water resources

USGS,
12201 Sunrise Valley Drive, Reston, VA 20192
Phone: (703) 648-4000
Website: http://water.usgs.gov

Wetlands International

Wetlands International is the only global non-governmental organization dedicated to the conservation of wetlands.

PO Box 471,
6700 AL Wageningen,
The Netherlands   Phone: +31 (0)317 478854
Website: www.wetlands.org

Xeriscape Colorado

Xeriscape™ Colorado is a program of the Colorado WaterWise Council and provides comprehensive information on drought-resistant gardening.

PO Box 40202, Denver, CO 80204-0202
Phone: (303) 893-2992
Website: www.xeriscape.org

THE CHELSEA GREEN GUIDES

CHELSEA GREEN'S NEW *GREEN GUIDES* are perfect tutors for consumers or businesses looking to green up their knowledge. Each compact, value-priced guide is packed with triple-bottom-line tips that will improve the environment and your finances. Slim enough to fit in a kitchen or desk drawer, you'll return to *The Chelsea Green Guides* frequently for concise, sage advice.

Energy: Use Less – Save More
JON CLIFT and
AMANDA CUTHBERT
9781933392721
$7.95

Composting: An Easy Household Guide
NICKY SCOTT
9781933392745
$7.95

Reduce, Reuse, Recycle: An Easy Household Guide
NICKY SCOTT
9781933392752
$7.95

If you enjoyed *Water: Use Less — Save More* please consider these other great *Green Guides* from Chelsea Green Publishing. To place an order please visit **www.chelseagreen.com** or call **802.295.6300**.